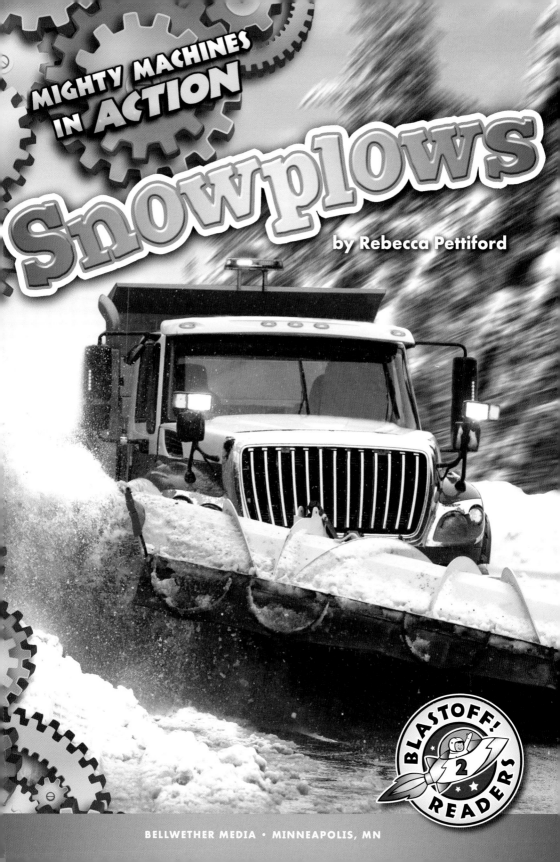

MIGHTY MACHINES IN ACTION

Snowplows

by Rebecca Pettiford

BLASTOFF! 2 READERS

BELLWETHER MEDIA · MINNEAPOLIS, MN

Note to Librarians, Teachers, and Parents:

Blastoff! Readers are carefully developed by literacy experts and combine standards-based content with developmentally appropriate text.

Level 1 provides the most support through repetition of high-frequency words, light text, predictable sentence patterns, and strong visual support.

Level 2 offers early readers a bit more challenge through varied simple sentences, increased text load, and less repetition of high-frequency words.

Level 3 advances early-fluent readers toward fluency through increased text and concept load, less reliance on visuals, longer sentences, and more literary language.

Level 4 builds reading stamina by providing more text per page, increased use of punctuation, greater variation in sentence patterns, and increasingly challenging vocabulary.

Level 5 encourages children to move from "learning to read" to "reading to learn" by providing even more text, varied writing styles, and less familiar topics.

Whichever book is right for your reader, Blastoff! Readers are the perfect books to build confidence and encourage a love of reading that will last a lifetime!

This edition first published in 2018 by Bellwether Media, Inc.

No part of this publication may be reproduced in whole or in part without written permission of the publisher. For information regarding permission, write to Bellwether Media, Inc., Attention: Permissions Department, 5357 Penn Avenue South, Minneapolis, MN 55419.

Library of Congress Cataloging-in-Publication Data

Names: Pettiford, Rebecca, author.
Title: Snowplows / by Rebecca Pettiford.
Description: Minneapolis, MN : Bellwether Media, Inc., [2018] | Series: Blastoff! Readers. Mighty Machines in Action | Includes bibliographical references and index. | Audience: Grades K-3. | Audience: Ages 5-8.
Identifiers: LCCN 2016052733 (print) | LCCN 2016055667 (ebook) | ISBN 9781626176331 (hardcover : alk. paper) | ISBN 9781681033631 (ebook)
Subjects: LCSH: Snowplows–Juvenile literature. | Snow removal–Juvenile literature.
Classification: LCC TD868 .P48 2018 (print) | LCC TD868 (ebook) | DDC 625.7/63–dc23
LC record available at https://lccn.loc.gov/2016052733

Text copyright © 2018 by Bellwether Media, Inc. BLASTOFF! READERS and associated logos are trademarks and/or registered trademarks of Bellwether Media, Inc. SCHOLASTIC, CHILDREN'S PRESS, and associated logos are trademarks and/or registered trademarks of Scholastic Inc.

Editor: Christina Leighton   Designer: Steve Porter

Printed in the United States of America, North Mankato, MN.

Table of **Contents**

WINTER WORKERS

Snow is falling fast.
A snowplow comes
down the icy street.

cab

The driver carefully steers from the **cab**.

salt

The snowplow pushes snow off the road. It also **scrapes** ice and lays salt.

Soon, the road is clear for everyone!

airport snowplow

Snowplows clear roads and sidewalks. They also plow parking lots.

Some of the biggest snowplows are at airports! They push snow off runways.

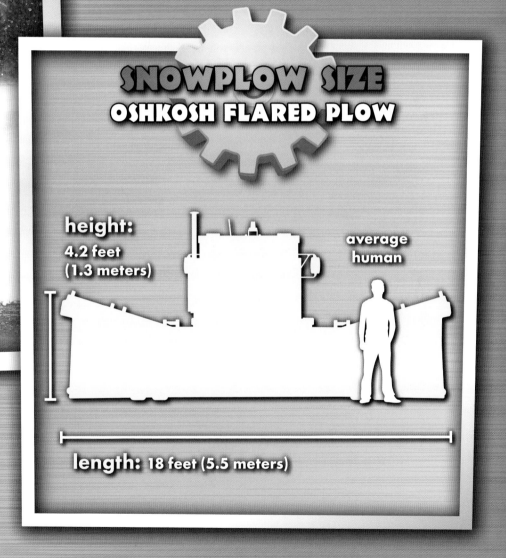

SNOWPLOW SIZE
OSHKOSH FLARED PLOW

height:
4.2 feet
(1.3 meters)

average human

length: 18 feet (5.5 meters)

Snowplows have many different body types.

COMMON SNOWPLOW BODY TYPES

four-wheeler/ATV

dump truck

loader

pickup truck

grader

They can be **pickup trucks** or **four-wheelers**. They can also be dump trucks or other big machines.

BLADES, HEADLIGHTS, AND SPREADERS

Snowplow **blades** come in different shapes.

straight blade

v-shaped blade

Straight blades push snow forward or off to one side. V-shaped blades push snow to both sides.

Some snowplows have blades that **scoop**. These can lift and move snow.

scoop

wing blade

Snowplows may have side blades called **wings**. These move even more snow!

Snowplows can have scraper blades under their bodies. These shave leftover snow and ice.

scraper blade

headlights

Headlights are on the front of snowplows. These shine through snowy weather.

spreader

Some snowplows have
spreaders. These spray
salt or sand onto the road.

The salt helps melt the ice. The sand makes the road less **slippery**.

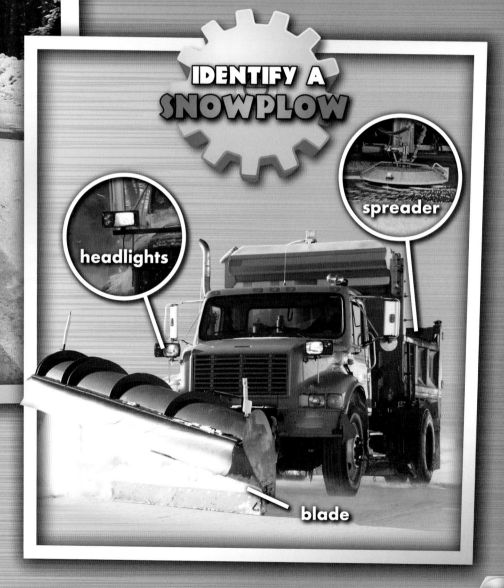

IDENTIFY A SNOWPLOW

spreader

headlights

blade

Snowplows make roads and neighborhoods safer in winter.

Without snowplows, winter travel would be much harder!

Glossary

blades—large metal plates that work like shovels

cab—the part of a snowplow where the driver sits

four-wheelers—small vehicles with four big wheels used on all types of ground; four-wheelers are also called all-terrain vehicles, or ATVs.

headlights—lights on the front of vehicles to light up the path ahead

pickup trucks—trucks with closed-off cabs and open backs

scoop—to pick up and move

scrapes—makes a surface smooth or clean with an edged tool

slippery—causing something to slide or fall

spreaders—attachments used to spread salt or sand over a wide area

wings—blades on the side of a snowplow

To Learn More

AT THE LIBRARY

Abbot, Henry. *I Want to Drive a Snowplow.*
New York, N.Y.: PowerKids Press, 2017.

Meister, Cari. *Snowplows.* Minneapolis,
Minn.: Bullfrog Books, 2017.

Oachs, Emily Rose. *Dump Trucks.* Minneapolis,
Minn.: Bellwether Media, 2017.

ON THE WEB

Learning more about snowplows
is as easy as 1, 2, 3.

1. Go to www.factsurfer.com.

2. Enter "snowplows" into the search box.

3. Click the "Surf" button and you will see a
   list of related web sites.

With factsurfer.com, finding more
information is just a click away.

Index

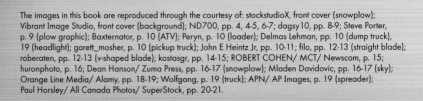